Original title:
Sculpted Lines

Author: Thor Castlebury
ISBN HARDBACK: 978-9916-88-086-9
ISBN PAPERBACK: 978-9916-88-087-6

The Delicate Craft

In the quiet of dusk, the hands create,
Shapes of dreams, carefully innate.
Whispers of color on canvas laid,
Each stroke tells tales, where hopes cascade.

Threads entwined in rhythmic dance,
Needles weave stories, a delicate chance.
Fabrications born from love and care,
In each pattern, a moment laid bare.

Molded by time, like soft clay bends,
Artistry blooms, where passion transcends.
Voices of silence, in harmony blend,
Crafting an echo, that never will end.

From thoughts to forms, the journey unfolds,
A tapestry rich, with secrets untold.
In the delicate craft, hearts intertwine,
Creating a world where dreams brightly shine.

Lines of Kindred Spirits

In the quiet glow of evening's light,
We share our dreams, taking flight.
Words weave softly, like threads of gold,
Binding hearts, a tale retold.

Laughter dances on the breeze,
Whispers flow with perfect ease.
Each smile a mirror, bright and clear,
Reflecting love, forever near.

Time may change the paths we tread,
But kindred spirits are never led.
In this bond, our souls entwined,
Finding solace, deeply aligned.

Emotive Profiles

Faces marked by joy and grief,
Stories crafted, beyond belief.
Each wrinkle holds a tale profound,
Silent echoes in beauty found.

Eyes that sparkle with endless dreams,
Painted in life's vibrant schemes.
A portrait speaks without a sound,
In hues of love, our hearts are found.

Through the shadows and the light,
We navigate both day and night.
Emotive profiles, a gallery true,
Reflecting all, both me and you.

The Mold of Memory

Memories cast in fragile clay,
Shaped by moments that fade away.
Each touch a mark, each laugh a line,
Carved in time, your heart in mine.

Fleeting shadows, lingering light,
Fragments dance in the depths of night.
In the silence, we hear their sound,
Whispers of love, forever bound.

Sculpted dreams and whispered sighs,
In the mold where our essence lies.
Through the years, we'll mold anew,
Crafting memories, me and you.

Crafted in Light

Sunrise paints the skies anew,
With every hue, a dream comes true.
Light cascades on paths we walk,
In silence, shadows start to talk.

Moments captured, glimmers bright,
Each click of time, a dance of light.
Crafted visions, we hold dear,
In the radiance, love draws near.

Together we shine, a radiant pair,
Illuminating truths laid bare.
In every heartbeat, we ignite,
A world reborn, crafted in light.

Breathing Life into Stillness

In the quiet, whispers dwell,
Filling spaces where shadows fell.
Hopes like dandelions take their flight,
Carried softly into the night.

Gentle breezes stir the air,
Awakening dreams, tender and rare.
Time stretches, soft and slow,
In stillness, the heart learns to grow.

Rustling leaves speak of change,
Each moment, sweet and strange.
Breath flows like a river's song,
In solitude, where we belong.

Reshaped Realities

Minds collide, ideas ignite,
Forming worlds in shared twilight.
Each thought a brush, strokes aligned,
Creating tapestries unconfined.

Infinite paths spiral and twist,
Dreams emerge from the mist.
Echoes of what could yet be,
In the heart's vast, boundless sea.

Shattered norms, a canvas bare,
New visions blossom in the air.
Every challenge a chance to see,
How beautiful change can be.

The Art of Embrace

Open arms in the morning light,
Welcoming warmth, chasing the night.
Connection blooms from heart to heart,
In unity, we find our part.

Gentle moments, tender and clear,
Whispered vows, a promise near.
Together we dance, souls entwined,
In the depths of love, we find.

Burdens shared, laughter rings,
In this bond, true freedom sings.
Hand in hand, we face the day,
The art of embrace leads the way.

Lines of Intention

Ink flows softly on the page,
Crafting dreams from heart's age.
Each stroke a step, a path to tread,
Words of purpose gently spread.

Navigating through thick and thin,
Mapping the places we have been.
Intentions drawn with clarity bright,
Illuminating the darkest night.

In the quiet, we find our way,
Lines of intention guide the day.
With courage bold, we take our stand,
Writing futures, hand in hand.

Designed Disturbances

In shadows cast by fleeting dreams,
A chaos blooms where silence screams.
The edges bend, the colors clash,
A symphony of discord's dash.

Whispers weave through tangled wires,
Fractured shapes, like wild desires.
Each heartbeat echoes in the night,
A dance of wrongs that feels so right.

Echoes of Structure

In rigid lines, a world takes shape,
Each corner turned, the mind escapes.
The framework holds a vibrant core,
A structured dance we can't ignore.

The rhythm pulses through the air,
A harmony of soft despair.
With every edge, a story's told,
In patterns new, the past unfolds.

Timeless Forms

In ancient stones, the stories lie,
A whisper of the wind's soft sigh.
The arches rise, defying time,
Each curve a note, each line a rhyme.

The sculptures breathe, their essence vast,
In frozen grace, a memory cast.
A silent ode to life's embrace,
In every form, a sacred space.

Crafted Reverie

In dreams we weave a tapestry,
Bright threads of hope, wild fancy free.
With careful hands, we shape our fate,
In peaceful realms where love can wait.

The gentle hum of thoughts in bloom,
A fragrant peace, dispelling gloom.
Each whispered wish, a starry flight,
In crafted dreams, we find our light.

Ellipses in Time

Moments drift like autumn leaves,
Fleeting whispers in the breeze.
Chronicles of days gone by,
Echoes dance beneath the sky.

Shadows stretch as sun descends,
Silent stories never end.
Fragments woven, soft and grand,
Each second slips like grains of sand.

The Language of Expression

Words collide in vibrant hues,
Crafting tales the heart can use.
Silence speaks when voices fade,
Emotions weave the paths we've laid.

Brushstrokes paint the dreams we chase,
In our souls, we find our place.
Every heartbeat softly sighs,
In the depths, true meaning lies.

Shapes of Solitude

In the quiet, shadows grow,
Moonlight casts a gentle glow.
Thoughts take flight on wings of night,
Finding solace, pure delight.

Echoes linger, soft and clear,
Whispered secrets only near.
In the stillness, hearts unite,
Shapes of solitude ignite.

Defined by Touch

Fingers graze in tender glow,
Every stroke a tale to show.
Softly woven through the night,
Hearts embrace in purest light.

Connections spark in silent space,
Every moment, time we trace.
In the warmth, we find our way,
Defined by touch, come what may.

Curves in Time

Time flows gently like a stream,
Winding paths of day and dream.
Moments twist and softly sway,
In the dance of night and day.

Whispers echo through the air,
Silent paths of joys and cares.
Curves that shape what we become,
In the rhythm, life is sung.

Etched Emotions

In the heart, a story grows,
Written deep where no one goes.
Etched in feelings, soft and bright,
Colors blending in the night.

Joy and sorrow intertwine,
Crafting moments, pure and fine.
Every tear, a tale unfurls,
A tapestry of inner worlds.

Shadows of Form

Silhouettes dance on the wall,
Casting shadows, large and small.
The shapes of thoughts, so undefined,
A fleeting glimpse of what we find.

In the silence, forms appear,
Echoes lingering, drawing near.
Whispered secrets, dark and bright,
In shadows, we reclaim the light.

The Geometry of Breath

Inhale the world, a sacred measure,
Exhale dreams, a hidden treasure.
Lines and angles form the way,
In the stillness, we convey.

Each breath a map of life we trace,
Finding solace in this space.
Geometry of hope and fear,
In every heartbeat, we draw near.

The Ballet of Stone

In silence, the stone begins to sway,
A dance of stillness, both firm and gray.
Whispers of time in each silent turn,
A figure of grace, in dusk it yearns.

Lifetimes etched in granite and clay,
The earth, a stage where shadows play.
Each crack a story, each chip a tune,
Ballet of nature beneath the moon.

Vessels of Thought

Thoughts drift like clouds, light and free,
Floating softly, like a euphony.
In the mind's eye, they form and dissolve,
Mysteries deep, waiting to evolve.

A vessel of dreams, it journeys afar,
Carrying echoes of who we are.
Reflections of souls in twilight's grace,
Waves of the heart in an endless chase.

Contours of the Heart

Each beat a whisper, each pulse a sigh,
Contours that bend beneath the sky.
The map of emotions, both soft and stark,
Tracing the journey from light to dark.

In shadows and light, the heart reveals,
The tapestry woven with joy and appeals.
Twists of longing, curves of pain,
A portrait of self in love's sweet rain.

Balancing Act

Life is a tightrope, balanced and frail,
A dance on the edge, a story to unveil.
With hope as our guide, we step from the ledge,
Twirling in grace on a fragile edge.

Each moment a choice, each breath a feat,
Navigating paths where fear and joy meet.
In the juggling act of what we are,
We find our balance, like a shining star.

The Palette of Existence

Life paints in hues so bright,
Each moment a brushstroke light.
In laughter and in tears we blend,
A canvas of colors that never end.

From dawn's blush to twilight's gleam,
We find ourselves in every dream.
The shades of love and shadows of fear,
All captured in this journey dear.

Through the storms our hearts reveal,
A tapestry of what we feel.
In every hue, our stories flow,
In the palette of life, we grow.

With vibrant strokes, we pave the way,
Creating art in the light of day.
Each color a heartbeat, a tale to tell,
In the palette of existence, we dwell.

In Carved Shadows

In the silence where echoes dwell,
Carved shadows whisper tales to tell.
The night drapes its cloak so deep,
Guarding secrets the heart will keep.

Under the moon's watchful gaze,
Figures dance in a twilight haze.
Embers glow and flicker bright,
Telling stories lost to night.

Each contour holds a memory dear,
In carved shadows we face our fear.
The past entwined with dreams anew,
A canvas of nights that we once knew.

In the stillness, reflections gleam,
In carved shadows, we chase a dream.
A testament to each silent sigh,
In the shadows, our spirits fly.

Impressions on the Soul

Each glance we share, a print we make,
In moments fleeting, hearts awake.
Impressions linger on pathways wide,
Marking the journey, side by side.

With the kindness of a simple smile,
We trace our journey, mile by mile.
Every encounter, a gentle touch,
Leaving imprints that mean so much.

In the silence, where thoughts reside,
Fleeting shadows no longer hide.
The patterns made by love's embrace,
Impressions drawing us to grace.

Through the years, like softest sand,
We shape our futures, hand in hand.
In the tapestry of life we weave,
Impressions on the soul, we believe.

Fractured Beauty

In twilight's glow, we find the way,
Fractured beauty in disarray.
Shattered dreams like scattered glass,
Reflecting moments, fading fast.

With every crack, a story told,
In broken pieces, hearts grown bold.
The imperfections sing their song,
In the chaos, we still belong.

Through the jagged edges we discover,
Strength in flaws, like no other.
In the fragments, we find our grace,
Fractured beauty, our saving space.

Amidst the wreckage, a light shines through,
Every fissure, a glimpse of truth.
In this mosaic, we learn to see,
Fractured beauty, setting us free.

Formed by Touch

In the silence, fingers dance,
Creating beauty by chance.
Softly molding, gentle sway,
Artisans shape the clay of day.

With each brush, a story unfolds,
Whispers of warmth in the molds.
Contours shifting in tender grace,
Embracing light in every space.

The heart reflects the tender art,
Formed by touch, where love can start.
In every curve, a memory glows,
In the hands, the spirit flows.

As twilight drapes the world in hush,
Life's creation sings in a rush.
Touched by hands that understand,
Together crafted, hand in hand.

Chiseled Dreams

In stone we find our wildest hopes,
Chiseled dreams on hopeful slopes.
Every stroke a tale untold,
Life's ambitions carved in bold.

With hammer’s grace, the artists play,
Revealing visions locked away.
Each chip falls like whispered truth,
Unraveling the threads of youth.

From solid rock, the figures rise,
A dance of dreams beneath the skies.
Chiseled paths through time's embrace,
Molding fate in a timeless space.

In shadows cast by work and art,
The yearning whispers from the heart.
Chiseled dreams will find their way,
In the light of each new day.

Contours of the Heart

Lines etched deep on tender skin,
Contours drawn where love begins.
Every curve tells a sweet refrain,
A map where joy and sorrow reign.

With every pulse, the shapes combine,
Twisting feelings, soft and fine.
Awakening in moonlit nights,
The heart reveals its hidden sights.

In gentle breaths, the whispers flow,
Contours shifting, love will grow.
Each embrace, a story spun,
In the twilight, two become one.

Tracing paths where shadows play,
In the quiet, we find our way.
Contours deepening, ever true,
The heart's embrace, me and you.

Shadows in the Stone

In empty corridors of time,
Shadows linger, soft and sublime.
Carved by hands of ancients past,
Whispering secrets that will last.

In solitude, the echoes sound,
A tale of beauty, lost then found.
Fragments linger in twilight's glow,
Shadows dancing, ebb and flow.

The stone remembers every tear,
Whispers of joy, and times of fear.
Each shadow paints a life once known,
In the silence, we feel it grown.

As darkness wraps the world in dreams,
The past reflects in gentle streams.
Shadows in stone, we find the thread,
Connecting hearts, though years have fled.

Grace in the Grain

In fields where whispers gently sway, The sun bestows its warm embrace, Each blade of grass, in light, will play, A dance of dark and softened grace.

The earth beneath, so rich and deep, Keeps secrets held in silent lore, While nature's pulse begins to leap, Life's stories told forevermore.

With every turn, a cycle blooms, The seasons cast a vivid role, Amidst the joy, the quiet glooms, Each moment shapes the heart and soul.

And so we cherish, tend, and weave, The threads of life in tender care, For every breath, we will believe, In grace that lingers everywhere.

Rhythm of the Mold

In shadows cast where edges blend, A quiet pulse begins to thrum, Each pattern formed, a tale to send, A symphony of life to come.

The clay beneath our fingertips, We shape and sculpt, with gentle hands, As dreams emerge from youth’s soft lips, The heart creates, the spirit stands.

Through time's embrace, the molds evolve, Each crack and line, a journey shown, In every form, our tales resolve, With rhythm rich, the past is sown.

In unity, we rise and bend, Together in this dance of fate, The rhythm calls, a timeless friend, In every mold, we celebrate.

Curved Conversations

In whispered tones, the echoes flow, Ideas twist like vines that cling, Beneath the stars, our thoughts will glow, In shadows deep, our voices sing.

Through winding paths of heart and mind, We share our hopes, our fears laid bare, In every pause, new truths we find, A tapestry of love to share.

With laughter bright, the moments bend, Each story told with tender care, Curved conversations never end, They linger softly in the air.

And as we speak, we intertwine, Our essence woven, strong and true, In every word, a sacred line, Connecting hearts in all we do.

Figures of Resilience

From ashes born, we rise anew, The scars we bear, a badge of grace, In storms we face, our strength shines through, Figures formed by time and space.

With each fall down, we learn to stand, The journey carved in silent tears, We stretch like roots beneath the sand, Resilience blooms across the years.

In shadows dark, we find the light, The will to grow, to push, to strive, We lift our heads, embrace the fight, In unity, we come alive.

Together, we are not alone, Each heart a beacon, strong and bold, In every challenge, seeds are sown, Figures of resilience unfold.

Textures of Emotion

Soft whispers linger, shadows dance,
Colors entwine in a fleeting glance.
Waves of joy, tides of despair,
Every heartbeat is tenderly bare.

Threads of laughter weave through the night,
In every sorrow, a flicker of light.
Frayed edges hold stories untold,
In the fabric of feelings, subtle and bold.

Textures of longing, smooth or coarse,
A tapestry woven from nature's course.
Each stitch a moment, each knot a sigh,
In the art of emotion, we live and die.

Nature's embrace, a comforting quilt,
Layered with warmth, our fears are spilt.
Emotions like seasons, ever in flow,
In the garden of longing, love starts to grow.

Carving the Void

In silence we shape what’s left unsaid,
Chiseling thoughts from the edge of dread.
A sculptor of shadows, hands cold and free,
Crafting the spaces where dreams wish to be.

Between the echoes of what could have been,
Lies the beauty of hope, paper thin.
Carving the void with a delicate hand,
Sculpting the silence, a fragile strand.

Chipping away at the weight of the night,
Etching the stars into soft morning light.
In every omission, a story unfolds,
A whisper of longing, a secret retold.

With patience and grace, we carve our path,
Transforming the void from bitterness to laugh.
In the depths of absence, creation thrives,
Life's art is the void from which love derives.

Formed from Fragments

Scattered pieces beneath our feet,
Hearts stitched together, fragile and sweet.
We gather the shards, in colors they gleam,
Formed from fragments, we craft a dream.

Each broken part tells a tale of its own,
In the chaos of life, our strength is shown.
We rise like a phoenix from ashes and dust,
In the fragments of sorrow, we learn to trust.

Life's mosaic, a dance of delight,
In every detail, darkness and light.
Formed from fragments, a beautiful mess,
In the art of existence, we find our progress.

With hands intertwined, we piece together,
A symphony played in all kinds of weather.
For in our collection of stories unclaimed,
Lies the beauty of life, ever unnamed.

Elegy of the Edges

At the brink of dusk, a sigh drifts low,
Whispers of memories in the gentle glow.
Edges of time blur like a fading song,
In the elegy of moments, we all belong.

Frayed at the seams, yet beautifully whole,
Carrying burdens, cradling the soul.
In quiet farewell, the night takes its stage,
An elegy written on each turning page.

Haunted by echoes of what used to be,
The edges of dreams whisper tenderly.
A tapestry woven of love and of loss,
An elegy sung, no matter the cost.

In the stillness of twilight, we find our grace,
The edges of life always leave a trace.
With each soft farewell, a new dawn we find,
A dance of the edges where souls are entwined.

A Dance with the Chisel

In hands of stone, the vision forms,
A dance unfolds where silence warms.
The chisel glides, a gentle breath,
Carving life from the cold, dark depth.

Each tap reveals the soul within,
Chiseling dreams from where they've been.
A rhythm born in dust and stone,
Creating beauty that feels like home.

Fingers coax the silent grace,
Each curve and line finds its place.
A world unfolds beneath the hand,
In sculpted whispers, tall and grand.

The dance is slow, yet time it flies,
In every stroke, a piece of skies.
A chisel's song the heart understands,
A timeless tale from skilled, strong hands.

The Contour of Memory

Fleeting moments echo past,
In shadows long, their traces cast.
A fragile line where dreams reside,
The contour of memory, like a tide.

Soft whispers float on evening air,
In hazy light, a whispered prayer.
Each faded thought, a star's embrace,
Lost in the labyrinth of time and space.

We wander through the paths we know,
In nostalgia's grip, we ebb and flow.
A gentle brush against the mind,
In memories lost, a solace we find.

The heart recalls what eyes can't see,
In fragile forms of what used to be.
A canvas painted with shades of past,
The contour of memory, forever cast.

Whispers Beneath the Surface

Ripples dance on tranquil seas,
Secrets hum in the gentle breeze.
Beneath the calm, the stories stir,
Whispers intertwine, a silent purr.

From depths unknown, they softly rise,
Tales of heartache and sweet goodbyes.
In currents deep, where shadows lay,
Life's essence flows in a muted ballet.

The moonlight glints on starlit dreams,
Reflecting truth in silent streams.
Beneath the surface, worlds collide,
In whispered tones, our souls confide.

Listen close to the ebb and flow,
To the whispers where the heartbeats glow.
For in the hush of night’s embrace,
Lie secrets wrapped in time and space.

Polished Reflections

In the glass, the world is found,
Edges sharp, with light profound.
Each polished surface, crisp and clear,
Reflects the thoughts we hold so dear.

We gaze upon our mirrored fate,
In silence deep, we contemplate.
The image shifts with every breath,
A dance of life that flirts with death.

Mirrored truths, we face the light,
In shadows dwell the fears of night.
But still, we search for clarity,
In polished reflections, we find glee.

Through every crack, the light will seep,
In fractured dreams, we learn to leap.
Polished reflections, both bright and stark,
Illuminate the paths we embark.

Sculpture of the Mind

Thoughts take shape in silent halls,
Ideas rise where shadows fall.
Chisels mark the lines we trace,
In the quiet, find our place.

Emerging forms, like dreams awake,
Flesh and spirit, not to break.
Beauty forged in inner strife,
Carved by the hands of our life.

Fragments whisper stories told,
Chiseled heart, both brave and bold.
Minds entwined in a dance so fine,
Crafting visions, our own design.

Artistry of thoughts combined,
Every echo, deeply lined.
In this space, let freedom gleam,
Sculpture made from purest dream.

Reflections of the Soul

In still waters, truths expand,
Glimmers dance with softest hand.
Each ripple tells a silent tale,
Of hearts that wander, love that sails.

Mirror glances, deep and wide,
Secrets kept, our hearts confide.
Whispers linger on the breeze,
Echoes of what we believe.

Softly time unveils its grace,
Lighting up a hidden space.
Every glance, a fleeting chance,
In the depths, we find our dance.

In reflections, shadows play,
Guiding us along the way.
Soul's mosaic, bright and whole,
A tapestry, the heart and soul.

Ebb and Flow

Waves of time, they rise and break,
Rhythms pulse for hearts that ache.
Tides that draw, yet push away,
Life's gentle touch, night and day.

Moments drift like autumn leaves,
Carried forth by whispering eaves.
In the stillness, echoes hum,
Reminding us where we are from.

Through the cycles, we will learn,
Holding close what we can turn.
Every ebb brings a new flow,
A chance to rise, a chance to grow.

In this dance of give and take,
Find the strength to bend, not break.
Let the rhythms guide your way,
Embrace the night, welcome the day.

Elegance in the Carving

With gentle touch of skilled design,
Stone gives way to pure divine.
Every curve tells tales of grace,
Time etches in a sacred space.

Crafted hands bring forth the light,
In the darkness, dreams ignite.
Chiseled faces, soft and bold,
Whispers of the ages told.

Beauty borne through every strike,
Echoing in every hike.
As layers fall, new shapes will rise,
Elegance in every guise.

In these forms, allow the soul,
To flourish, stretch, and be whole.
For in the art of carving fine,
We find the heart where worlds align.

A Tapestry of Touch

In gentle threads of silken grace,
The warmth of souls begins to trace.
With every fold, a story spun,
A dance of hearts, two becoming one.

The fibers weave through laughter's song,
In tender moments, where we belong.
Each stitch, a memory held so tight,
A tapestry of love, pure and bright.

Across the canvas, colors blend,
In every corner, love transcends.
A masterpiece so warmly sought,
In the tapestry of touch, we're caught.

So let us stitch with care and time,
A fabric rich, a love sublime.
In every thread, a soft embrace,
Together, we create our space.

Carving Tomorrow

With chisel poised and heart aflame,
We carve our dreams, we make our claim.
In every stroke, a vision clear,
Crafting futures, free from fear.

The marble waits, so cold and stark,
Yet in its veins, there lies a spark.
With hands that shape and mold the clay,
We sculpt our hopes, come what may.

Through sweat and toil, we forge ahead,
In every step, our fears we shed.
The day will break, the dawn will call,
Together, we shall rise, never fall.

So let us carve, with strength and grace,
A tomorrow bright, a sacred space.
In the art of time, we'll find our way,
Creating life, day by day.

Celestial Contours

In twilight's glow, the stars align,
Silhouettes against the sky's design.
Celestial whispers, soft and clear,
We trace the night, with dreams sincere.

The moon, a guide, through darkened seas,
Unfolds the night with gentle ease.
Each constellation, a story told,
In silver threads, the past unfolds.

We map the heavens, inked in light,
A dance of time, a cosmic flight.
Through stellar paths, our spirits glide,
In celestial contours, we abide.

So lift your gaze, embrace the night,
In every twinkle, find your light.
For in the cosmos, vast and grand,
Together, we will take our stand.

In the Hands of Time

Time flows gently, like a stream,
Winding softly, shaping dreams.
Each tick, a sigh, a breath we take,
In the hands of time, our hearts awake.

With every moment, shadows dance,
A fleeting glance, a whispered chance.
In the cradle of this timeless space,
We find our rhythm, we find our place.

As seasons change and flowers bloom,
In the cycle, we all find room.
Through every sunrise, every dusk,
In the hands of time, we place our trust.

So let us cherish, every beat,
In this journey, bittersweet.
For in the hands of time, we'll find,
A tapestry of life, intertwined.

Etched in Time

Moments linger like shadows' grace,
Memories woven in the fabric of space.
Each heartbeat a whisper, soft and sublime,
Life's fleeting essence, etched deep in time.

Seasons shift like the tides that flow,
Flowers bloom and fade, yet beauty grows.
With every dawn, new stories align,
In the tapestry of life, love's design.

Faces fade but spirits remain,
In the echoes of laughter, joy, and pain.
Through the ages, we dance, we rhyme,
Forever captured, we're etched in time.

The Shape of Longing

In the depths of night, a whisper calls,
Echoes of dreams in the shadowed halls.
Yearning hearts beat in a rhythm so fine,
A fragile desire, the shape of longing.

Stars twinkle softly, a guiding light,
Promises linger in the stillness of night.
Embers of hope leave a warm, sweet sign,
We reach for the future, in the shape of longing.

Paths intertwine like a gentle stream,
Chasing the whispers that beckon a dream.
In every heartbeat, in every line,
We find our solace, the shape of longing.

Carved in Silence

In the quiet hours, secrets unfold,
Whispers of stories yet to be told.
A moment of stillness, a breath divine,
Fragments of truth, carved deep in silence.

Beneath the surface, emotions reside,
In the hush of the night, they cannot hide.
Layers of time, like a fine wine,
Each note a memory, carved in silence.

Time flows gently, like clouds on the sea,
Holding our dreams in timeless decree.
In every pause, we intertwine,
The essence of life, carved in silence.

Embracing the Curve

Life's gentle bend, a softened grace,
Each twist a dance, each turn a trace.
In the rhythm of change, we find our groove,
Embracing the curve, we learn to move.

Mountains rise high, then gently slope,
With every step, we kindle hope.
In the winding paths, our dreams prove,
Love flourishes sweetly, embracing the curve.

Stars in the distance guide our way,
Through valleys of doubt, come what may.
With open hearts, we find our resolve,
In the dance of life, embracing the curve.

Molded Memories

In the clay of yesterday, we shape,
Contours of laughter, shadows escape.
Whispers of moments, tender and true,
Each crack a story, a part of our hue.

Fingers tracing paths on the old wall,
Imprints of joy, the rise and the fall.
Time is a sculptor, rough yet refined,
Carving our lives, intertwined and aligned.

Framed in the light of the fading sun,
Colors of dreams, now lost but not done.
Echoes resound in the silence we keep,
Molded by memories, alive in our sleep.

Fleeting like tides, they ebb and they flow,
Each shape a reminder of all we could know.
In the heart's gallery, portraits reside,
Molded by moments, forever our guide.

Angular Dreams

In a world of edges, sharp and defined,
We chase the corners, where visions unwind.
Every angle a promise, a path yet unknown,
In the structure of dreams, our spirits have grown.

Lines intersecting, with purpose they bind,
Drawing the hopeful, the brave, and the kind.
Angles of fortune, both peril and grace,
In the geometry of night, we find our place.

Fragments of starlight, refracted they gleam,
Cutting through shadows, igniting the beam.
Triangles whisper, of futures unspun,
In the lattice of life, we dance just begun.

Building our castles on peaks made of thought,
Sketching our stories in lessons we've sought.
With every sharp turn, we learn to believe,
In angular dreams, we grow and achieve.

Fluid Figures

In the dance of water, shapes take their flight,
Bending and swirling, lost in the night.
Figures arise from the depths of the sea,
Graceful and fleeting, they whisper to me.

Ripples of laughter, a soft gentle sound,
Flowing like currents that swirl all around.
Every motion, a story, a breath of the past,
In liquid embraces, we find freedom vast.

Colors are merging, the canvas runs free,
Creating a palette of who we can be.
Fluidity reigns in the heart of the tide,
Where figures of life and dreams coincide.

Sculpted by moments, both tender and wild,
Nature's own rhythm, forever beguiled.
In the rush of the currents, our spirits take flight,
Fluid figures of hope, in the deep of the night.

Whispered Silhouettes

In the hush of twilight, shadows take form,
Silhouettes speak softly, a bodiless norm.
Outlined in mystery, secrets they tell,
Ghosts of the past in a silent farewell.

Catching the whispers that dance through the air,
Figures of memory, tender and rare.
Each frame a story, each curve a refrain,
Whispered silhouettes call out our name.

Moonlight reveals what the day keeps concealed,
The depth of our dreams, now lovingly healed.
In the embrace of dusk, where time feels like fate,
Whispers of silhouettes guide us to relate.

Together we wander, hand in hand through the dark,
Finding our light in each quiet spark.
With every soft echo, a new path we set,
In whispered silhouettes, we never forget.

Embodied Whispers

In the hush of twilight, dreams entwine,
Soft voices call, a gentle sign.
The heart remembers, a silent tune,
Echoed whispers under the moon.

Each sigh a secret, softly shared,
Moments of love, tenderly bared.
Wander through shadows, lost but found,
In the stillness, connection unbound.

Through fragile silence, stories unfold,
In every glance, warmth turns bold.
A tapestry woven of heartbeats dear,
Whispers envelop, ever near.

Within the silence, souls unite,
In embodied whispers, pure delight.
Holding each story, vast and bright,
Infinite dreams in the fading light.

Stories in Silhouette

Shadows dance on the wall's embrace,
Figures of memories, time won't erase.
Each contour holds a moment dear,
Silhouettes whisper, loud and clear.

In twilight's glow, tales come alive,
Fragments of laughter, where we strive.
Flickers of light, shadows take flight,
Every outline tells of our fight.

Through the veils of dusk, we carve our fate,
Stories linger, we celebrate.
Joined in the chill of the falling night,
In shapes of hope, we find our light.

As dreams unfold in a silent show,
In every trace, the heart will know.
Stories in silhouette softly grow,
Echoing love as time moves slow.

Geometry of Affection

Angles meet, where hearts align,
In the space between, love does shine.
Circles drawn, infinite grace,
In each embrace, a sacred place.

Triangles form, sturdy and bold,
In shared moments, warmth unfolds.
Lines of connection, straight and true,
Each path we travel, me and you.

Shapes intertwine in a dance of fate,
Holding our dreams, we contemplate.
Symmetry found in laughter's ring,
In the geometry of affection, we sing.

Parallel lives, side by side,
Through all the angles, we confide.
In patterns drawn, love's design,
Together we grow, entwined, divine.

Traces of the Past

Footprints linger in the sand,
Memories whisper, hand in hand.
Faded echoes, old songs play,
In the heart's gallery, they stay.

Time weaves stories, shadows cast,
In every glance, we hold the past.
Fragments of laughter, tears we shed,
In the tapestry of what we've read.

Letters buried in weathered books,
Whispers of love, the way it looks.
Traces linger on whispered sighs,
In the story of us, forever ties.

Yet in the journey, we break new ground,
In every heartbeat, truth is found.
Though traces of the past may remain,
We shape the future from joy and pain.

Embedded Echoes

Whispers of the past, soft and clear,
They dance in the shadows, drawing near.
Memories linger, a haunting refrain,
Resonating deeply, like an ancient chain.

In chambers of silence, secrets reside,
Each flicker of thought, a gentle guide.
Echoes that ripple through time and space,
Revealing the essence we cannot trace.

Voices entwined in a timeless embrace,
The pulse of existence, a sacred base.
In every heartbeat, a story unfolds,
A tapestry woven from threads untold.

And here in the stillness, I find my way,
With echoes of wisdom that softly sway.
Embedded in moments, the past still glows,
In the heart's quiet chambers, the spirit knows.

Fluid Architecture

Waves of creation, flowing and free,
Structures emerge from the depths of the sea.
Curves intertwine, a delicate dance,
Building foundations, in a fleeting glance.

Each form evolves, a story untold,
Crafted from dreams, both tender and bold.
Colors that meld in a vibrant embrace,
A canvas of life, where visions trace.

Through fluid expressions, we shape our fate,
Breaking the boundaries that we create.
In the rhythm of change, we find our song,
An architecture of feelings, ever strong.

And as the tides shift, we learn to adapt,
In the fluidity, a beauty wrapped.
With every transition, new horizons bloom,
In the dance of creation, we find our room.

Forms of Desire

Flickers of longing in the depths of the soul,
Craving connections that make us whole.
Like shadows that stretch in the warm evening light,
Desires take shape, emerging from night.

In the silence of dreams, we dare to explore,
What lies beyond the horizon's door.
Touched by the magic of whispered breaths,
In the forms of desire, we conquer our depths.

Soft glances exchanged, electric and real,
In spirals of passion, the heart starts to feel.
Each moment a pulse, each touch a spark,
Illuminating pathways that once were dark.

As tides of emotion rise and they fall,
We navigate currents, surrendering all.
In the whirlpool of yearning, we find our place,
In the forms of desire, we embrace our grace.

The Heart's Blueprint

Lines etched by longing, a design so clear,
A map of our journeys, through joy and through fear.
Each heartbeat a marker, each breath an intent,
In the heart's blueprint, our spirits cement.

Layers of feeling, both fragile and strong,
Crafting a melody, an everlasting song.
With courage as ink, we sketch our own fate,
In the quiet of moments, we contemplate.

Through trials and triumphs, we navigate time,
In the depths of our essence, we seek the sublime.
For every connection, there's a path intertwined,
In the heart's blueprint, our truths we find.

And when shadows linger, we draw on this map,
With love as our compass, we close every gap.
In the tapestry woven, our lives intertwine,
The heart's blueprint whispers, forever divine.

Threads of Creation

In the loom of night, we weave,
Colors bright, chosen with care.
Whispers of starlight, we believe,
Creating patterns, rare and fair.

From the silence, visions rise,
Each thread a tale, softly spun.
In the depths, our spirit lies,
With every knot, a new day's begun.

Hope entwined in every stitch,
Woven tight, our dreams ignite.
Through the dark, we find the niche,
Threads of love, a guiding light.

In the tapestry of the soul,
Every hue tells where we’ve been.
Together, we make ourselves whole,
Threads of creation, timeless sheen.

The Heart's Sculptor

With gentle hands, the sculptor molds,
A heart of stone, once cold, now warm.
Chiseling dreams, as life unfolds,
Crafting love, a lasting charm.

Each strike echoes through the air,
Resonating with tender grace.
In every groove, a whispered prayer,
Caressing time, a warm embrace.

Through the marble, feelings flow,
Shapes of sorrow, joy, and strife.
The heart reveals what we can't show,
In each curve, the art of life.

The sculptor dreams with every beat,
Creating worlds in silent art.
In the end, our hearts repeat,
A masterpiece that plays its part.

Designing the Unfolded

Blueprints sketched in twilight's glow,
Plans of futures yet to see.
Lines and shapes that ebb and flow,
Designing paths for you and me.

Each fold a journey to embrace,
In every crease, a story lies.
We shape the void, create our space,
With open hearts, beneath the skies.

Colors splash against the gray,
Dreams emerge like petals bright.
In the chaos, find our way,
Design the day, ignite the night.

Together, we'll unfold the plan,
With each step, the world will see.
Crafting visions hand in hand,
Designing the beauty, you and me.

Geometry of Dreams

Angles sharp, like truths we seek,
Circles drawn around our fears.
In the silence, visions speak,
Mapping paths through laughter and tears.

Shapes collide in vibrant dance,
Triangles whisper of their fate.
In this art, we find our chance,
To embrace all, to love, create.

With every line, a dream takes flight,
Forms of hope across the void.
In geometry, we find our light,
The abstract world we once enjoyed.

Connect the dots, we'll find the way,
Through the patterns, life aligns.
In this space, hearts will sway,
The geometry of dreams unwinds.

In the Hands of Creation

In the dawn, whispers breathe soft,
Colors blend, dreams aloft.
Hands mold clay, visions arise,
A dance of life beneath the skies.

From the canvas, shadows spill,
Echoes of nature, strength and will.
Each stroke tells a story rare,
Crafted with love, tender care.

The world spins in a painter's heart,
Every moment, a brand new start.
In silence, the spark ignites,
Glimmers of hope, endless nights.

Creation's song, a gentle tide,
In each breath, spirits glide.
Weaving fate with threads so fine,
In the hands of creation, we shine.

Shapes of Solitude

In quiet corners, shadows play,
Figures linger, kept at bay.
Whispers echo in the void,
Where silence reigns, thoughts deployed.

Each shape holds a tale untold,
Reflections of a heart so bold.
The walls listen, secrets shared,
In solitude, hope is bared.

Waves of stillness softly crash,
Time retreats, a fleeting flash.
Embrace the silence, find the peace,
In shapes of solitude, release.

In the night, the stars align,
Each twinkle, a thought divine.
Amidst the dark, a light does bloom,
In shapes of solitude, find your room.

The Language of Texture

In every grain, a story dwells,
Rough or smooth, a magic spells.
Fingers trace the lines of time,
A tapestry, both raw and sublime.

Silk and stone, a dance of grace,
Ridges and folds, a warm embrace.
Hues collide, shadows play,
The language of texture leads the way.

Fractured edges, soft and pure,
A dialogue that's rich and sure.
With every touch, a world unfolds,
A symphony of both young and old.

In the weave of life's grand design,
Each texture speaks, a silent sign.
Listen close, let senses guide,
In the language of texture, abide.

Facets of Light

In the dawn, the world ignites,
Colors shimmer, pure delights.
Each ray bends, a story spun,
Facets dance, in morning sun.

Through leaves green, shadows play,
Whispers of dusk push night away.
In every spark, hope takes flight,
A kaleidoscope, facets of light.

Glimmers trace the path we roam,
A guide through darkness, leading home.
In every heart, a spark so bright,
Illuminates our shared insight.

As stars awaken, dreams take form,
In the night sky, a radiant swarm.
We are the echoes, shining bright,
Forever bound by facets of light.

Tactile Stories

Fingers trace the worn old page,
Each crease holds a tale untold,
Textures breathe the past anew,
In silence, whispers softly unfold.

The fabric of memory weaves,
Threads of joy, threads of pain,
Each stitch a moment captured,
A tapestry in the rain.

The warmth of scars beneath the skin,
Emotions sculpted, fierce and bold,
In every touch, the heart begins,
To write its story, brave and gold.

With every pulse, a life expressed,
A canvas rich with every sway,
Tactile stories linger deep,
In the dance of night and day.

Horizons of Possibility

Beyond the edge where skies embrace,
A whisper calls, to dare and dream,
Each dawn unveils a brand new space,
Where hopes take flight, like morning steam.

In every shadow, light can rise,
A chance to weave the world anew,
Each choice, a step, each wish, a prize,
Horizons call with vibrant hue.

From starlit paths to oceans wide,
The journey shapes through twists and turns,
With open hearts, let courage guide,
For in each heart, a fire burns.

Embrace the unknown, let it unfold,
With every heartbeat, let it flow,
Horizons stretch, a sight to behold,
In endless grace, where dreams will grow.

Curves of Emotion

In gentle arcs, the heart does sway,
A dance of feelings, soft and strong,
With every curve, a wordless play,
In silence, right where we belong.

Like rivers winding through the land,
Each bend reveals a deeper truth,
Flowing freely, hand in hand,
Through trials faced and moments smooth.

Wrapped in warmth, the shadows cling,
As laughter curves into the night,
A symphony that memories sing,
Composed of shadows, love, and light.

Curves of emotion, rich and deep,
Charting maps of what we feel,
In every sigh, a promise keeps,
The heart, a canvas, bold and real.

Whispers in the Clay

Fingers mold the earthen form,
With every push, a spirit wakes,
In whispers soft, creation born,
Through pulse and breath, the artist aches.

Shapes emerge from minds so vast,
Each piece a story, raw and true,
A dance of hands, a timeless cast,
In clay, our dreams begin anew.

The wheel spins on, a sacred dance,
As time dissolves in grains of sand,
We shape our hopes, we take our chance,
In every curve, our hearts expand.

Whispers carried in the clay,
A testament to where we've been,
In every pot, a story stays,
Embraced by hands, and souls within.

Captured Essence

In twilight's gentle glow, we find,
Moments frozen, thoughts entwined.
Whispers dance in fading light,
Memories linger, pure and bright.

A shimmer of laughter, a fleeting glance,
Each heartbeat holds its own romance.
Caught in the stillness, the world fades,
In these fragments, true life parades.

Colors bleed into the night sky,
Painting the stories of you and I.
Each breath a treasure, each sigh a song,
In this essence, we all belong.

Beyond the shadows, the truth remains,
Captured moments, joy and pains.
In the heart’s vault, they softly nest,
Essence of life, forever blessed.

Drafts of Creation

In silence, ideas softly bloom,
Sketching dreams in a quiet room.
Words like brushstrokes on a page,
Drafts of life, uncaged.

Each thought a seed, waiting to grow,
Imaginations flow like rivers below.
In hesitant lines, visions take flight,
Sketches of passion, pure delight.

Lines unravel, narratives weave,
In the chaos, a world to believe.
Dreams scribbled in margins embrace,
Building realms in time and space.

With every draft, we shape our fate,
Navigating dreams, we innovate.
From whispered thoughts to vivid scenes,
In the drafts, our spirit gleams.

Molded by Hands

With clay and care, forms begin,
Molded gently, the journey within.
Hands create magic in every touch,
Crafting beauty that means so much.

Textures rise and shadows play,
In their grasp, dreams find a way.
Each curve tells stories untold,
In every creation, warmth unfolds.

From earthy tones to glimmers bright,
Shapes emerge in the fading light.
Hearts entwined with every press,
In the art of making, there's a finesse.

Molded by hands, we find our place,
In every piece, a trace of grace.
Through effort and love, visions are spun,
In the act of creation, we become one.

Sculpting the Unseen

In shadows' depth, visions arise,
Sculpting the unseen, where silence lies.
Chisels whisper against the stone,
Revealing secrets once unknown.

Each strike a heartbeat, a pulse divine,
Carving the essence, the grand design.
Layers peeled back, in effort bestowed,
Unveiling wonders, in stillness flowed.

Fingers trace dreams in solitude,
Sculpting the fabric of life imbued.
As visions take shape, they breathe and sigh,
In the artistry crafted, we learn to fly.

Through patience and love, the unseen shows,
In every sculpture, life's beauty glows.
With each revealing, our spirits align,
Sculpting the unseen, a journey divine.

Unveiled Volumes

In shadows deep, the stories hide,
Whispers of dreams, in silence bide.
Pages turn with a gentle sigh,
Unlock the truths where secrets lie.

Ink stains flow like rivers wide,
Carrying tales, a heartfelt tide.
Each word crafted with careful grace,
Unveiling worlds in space and place.

Resonance in Relief

Echoes dance through silent halls,
Carried gently by evening calls.
In the quiet, hearts align,
Finding solace in the design.

Notes of peace, in whispers spread,
Resounding soft where fears have fled.
Harmony lingers, sweet and bright,
A balm for souls who seek the light.

The Etching of Existence

Time etches lines upon the face,
Stories woven with gentle grace.
Moments caught in fleeting breath,
Life's embrace, a dance with death.

In the echoes of laughter's glint,
Memories carved, the heart's imprint.
Each heartbeat marks the course we take,
In the etching of all we make.

Threads of Perception

Colors blend in the mind's embrace,
Threads of thoughts weave a tapestry's trace.
Wonders unfold in a whispered dream,
As reality bends at the seam.

Perceptions shift with each passing hour,
Like blossoms that reach for the sun's power.
In the fabric of life, we find our way,
Each thread a promise of a new day.

Cast in the Twilight

The sun dips low, a tender sigh,
Shadows stretch, as stars will pry.
Whispers of night begin to sing,
Drifting dreams on twilight's wing.

A canvas bright in fading light,
Hues of day blend into night.
Silhouettes dance in gentle breeze,
Nature's breath, a soft unease.

The moon ascends with silver grace,
In its glow, lost souls embrace.
Time stands still as dusk unfolds,
Secrets wrapped in twilight's folds.

In quiet moments, hearts align,
Casting wishes, ties divine.
Eternal hush where dreams ignite,
Forever held in cast of night.

The Archive of Shapes

In every corner, lines define,
A spectrum broad of forms divine.
The whispers here of curves and bends,
In stillness, art and thought transcends.

Pages worn with tales of old,
Each shape a story, softly told.
Fragments captured in their grace,
An endless search for sacred space.

From sharpest edge to gentle sway,
The archive breathes of night and day.
A tapestry of life unfolds,
In shifting shades, the heart beholds.

Through frames of whispers and soft light,
We navigate this silent night.
Shapes of longing, shapes of fate,
In this archive, we create.

Forming the Spirit

In every breath, a spark ignites,
A dance of shadows, whispers, sights.
Forming essences, soft and pure,
In quiet spaces, we endure.

Nature's voice, a guiding rhyme,
In unity, we carve through time.
Each heartbeat resonates a truth,
In forming spirit, lies our youth.

Through trials faced, through joys embraced,
In every moment, souls are traced.
Layer by layer, we define,
In sculpted thoughts, our fates entwine.

The journey winds like rivers flow,
In shaping depths, our spirits grow.
A canvas vast, each stroke a part,
In forming all, we find the heart.

Chiseled Delicacy

From rugged stone, the hands will carve,
Delicate dreams in shadows starve.
Each movement gentle, purpose clear,
In chiseled touch, we hold what's dear.

The beauty lies in flaws embraced,
In every mark, a life is traced.
Once heavy burdens now refined,
In sacred forms, our souls aligned.

Through ages past, the trial's grace,
A dance of time cannot erase.
In whispers soft, the heart reveals,
Chiseled delicacy, truth feels.

With every edge, a story breathes,
In careful craft, the spirit weaves.
A masterpiece of life displayed,
In chiseled love, forever laid.

Carved Whispers

In the forest, voices sway,
Echoes linger, then decay.
Wooden hearts, tales to tell,
Nature's secrets, cast a spell.

Shadows dance on ancient stone,
Silent tales of things unknown.
Each carved line, a heartbeat's pulse,
Whispers soft, the night convulse.

Fingers trace the bark and grain,
History etched in soft refrain.
Glimmers of light through leaves and vines,
Past and present intertwine.

In stillness found, the world takes pause,
Carved whispers hold the heart's applause.
Guiding souls with gentle grace,
Nature's art, a warm embrace.

Contours of Silence

In shadows deep, contours breathe,
A quiet space, the mind can weave.
Soft curves caress the edge of night,
Silent forms that hold the light.

Whispers echo in the gleam,
Murmurs blend with the moonbeam.
Every line, a gentle trace,
Contours hold the softest grace.

Time stands still in this embrace,
Moments held in sacred space.
In silence flows the tangled thread,
Contours guide where dreams are led.

Hidden truths beneath the skin,
Chasing shadows deep within.
Artistry found in quiet art,
Contours of silence, soft and smart.

Chiseled Grace

A statue poised in frozen time,
Chiseled grace in form and rhyme.
Every angle, a story told,
In quiet stone, the brave and bold.

Fingers carve through layers thick,
Each stroke, a gentle flick.
Shaped by hands that understand,
Art takes flight at their command.

Lines that mimic life's sweet flow,
Chiseled grace in ebb and glow.
Every crack, a tale that’s gleamed,
Artisan's dreams in whispers steamed.

In marble breathes the heart’s desire,
Crafted spirit touched by fire.
With patience born of love's embrace,
Eternity lives in chiseled grace.

The Art of Edges

Sharp and bold, the edges gleam,
Cutting through the softest dream.
In every line, a fierce intent,
The art of edges, time well spent.

Fractured light forms patterns bright,
Angles merge in the fading light.
Crafted whispers, a daring trace,
Every edge, a new embrace.

Precision found in raw design,
Edges peel back what's felt divine.
A subtle push, a gentle draw,
The magic held in each raw flaw.

Beauty lives where angles clash,
In the moments that flash and flash.
The art of edges tells the tale,
Holding truth in every veil.

Milton Keynes UK
Ingram Content Group UK Ltd.
UKHW032316121024
449481UK00011B/327

9 789916 880876